Sixth Grade Math Workbook

Ratios and Percent

Speedy Publishing LLC
40 E. Main St. #1156
Newark, DE 19711
www.speedypublishing.com

Change decimals to percents and vice versa

Write the following decimals as percents and vice versa, as indicated.

1. 74% =

2. 99% =

3. = 0.53

4. 86% =

5. = 0.77

6. = 0.39

7. 11% =

8. = 0.21

9. = 0.23

10. 82% =

11. 69% =

12. 58% =

13. 5% =

14. = 0.5

15. 63% =

16. = 0.69

17. 37% =

18. = 0.81

19. = 0.72

20. 76% =

21. = 0.49

22. 69% =

23. = 0.65

24. = 0.21

25. 30% =

26. = 0.1

27. = 0.13

28. 94% =

29. 46% =

30. 56% =

31. = 0.44

32. 45% =

33. = 0.28

34. 22% =

35. 9% =

36. = 0.57

37. 78% =

38. = 0.97

39. = 0.55

40. 60% =

41. 49% =

42. 51% =

43. = 0.77

44. 27% =

45. 26% =

46. 37% =

47. 31% =

48. 59% =

49. = 0.18

50. = 0.07

51. 71% =

52. = 0.06

53. 13% =

54. = 0.48

55. 92% =

56. 58% =

57. = 0.28

58. = 0.55

59. 3% =

60. 87% =

61. 32% =

62. = 0.6

63. = 0.16

64. 10% =

Find percentages of numbers

Calculate the percentages.

1. 50% of 110

2. 30% of 110

3. 50% of 130

4. 40% of 0

5. 60% of 150

6. 60% of 70

7. 50% of 20

8. 100% of 110

9. 80% of 80

10. 40% of 150

11. 90% of 0

12. 60% of 40

13. 70% of 0

14. 50% of 140

15. 50% of 100

16. 70% of 40

17. 70% of 40

18. 0% of 50

19. 40% of 50

20. 50% of 150

21. 10% of 90

22. 100% of 130

23. 80% of 70

24. 70% of 10

25. 50% of 10

26. 30% of 60

27. 70% of 90

28. 70% of 80

29. 70% of 30

30. 50% of 110

31. 20% of 110

32. 90% of 20

33. 100% of 66

34. 90% of 11

35. 100% of 106

36. 30% of 128

37. 30% of 72

38. 0% of 53

39. 10% of 136

40. 70% of 69

41. 30% of 99

42. 0% of 90

43. 20% of 19

44. 20% of 121

45. 90% of 134

46. 50% of 108

47. 90% of 148

48. 70% of 6

49. 37% of 59

50. 88% of 99

51. 90% of 26

52. 55% of 135

53. 77% of 102

54. 31% of 146

55. 48% of 111

56. 74% of 31

57. 65% of 111

58. 31% of 68

59. 42% of 146

60. 17% of 15

61. 61% of 72

62. 59% of 85

63. 33% of 54

64. 46% of 24

65. 6% of 22

66. 85% of 142

Find how many percent a number is of another

Solve.

1. How many percent of 100 is 50?

2. How many percent of 60 is 45?

3. 25 is what percentage of 50?

4. 60 is what percentage of 60?

5. How many percent of 80 is 10?

6. 25 is what percentage of 40?

7. How many percent of 45 is 10?

8. How many percent of 55 is 25?

9. How many percent of 60 is 50?

10. 10 is what percentage of 70?

11. How many percent of 100 is 20?

12. 10 is what percentage of 95?

13. How many percent of 20 is 10?

14. How many percent of 75 is 45?

15. 5 is what percentage of 30?

16. How many percent of 80 is 35?

17. 75 is what percentage of 90?

18. How many percent of 45 is 45?

19. 15 is what percentage of 50?

20. How many percent of 10 is 5?

21. How many percent of 100 is 70?

22. 50 is what percentage of 75?

23. 5 is what percentage of 55?

24. 5 is what percentage of 25?

25. 15 is what percentage of 85?

26. 40 is what percentage of 90?

Percentage Summary Worksheets

Solve.

1. What is 68% of 56?

2. 12 is what percentage of 24?

3. How many percent of 39 is 9?

4. How many percent of 72 is 13?

5. What is 32% of 63?

6. 8 is what percentage of 78?

7. 34 is what percentage of 85?

8. Find 27% of the number 86.

9. Find 41% of the number 45.

10. How many percent of 76 is 26?

11. What is 67% of 23?

12. What is 70% of 26?

13. What is 9% of 59?

14. Find 60% of the number 39.

15. 29 is what percentage of 89?

16. What is 54% of 21?

17. 2 is what percentage of 42?

18. What is 93% of 17?

19. What is 11% of 90?

20. 78 is what percentage of 99?

21. How many percent of 49 is 39?

22. How many percent of 76 is 40?

23. Find 73% of the number 21.

24. What is 63% of 40?

25. What is 73% of 19?

26. 1 is what percentage of 92?

27. How many percent of 46 is 2?

28. What is 49% of 61?

29. 53 is what percentage of 93?

30. What is 14% of 99?

31. Find 43% of the number 6.

32. Find 8% of the number 79.

33. What is 93% of 95?

Ratios

Reduce the following ratios.

1. 2:4 = ____________

2. 6:9 = ____________

3. 5:15 = ____________

4. 12:20 = ____________

5. 18:45 = ____________

6. 21:49 = ____________

7. 33:121 = ____________

8. 30:72 = ____________

9. 39:52 = ____________

10. 52:56 = ____________

11. 90:78 = ___________

12. 90:70 = ___________

13. 94:96 = ___________

14. 45:39 = ___________

15. 92:2 = ___________

16. 24:4 = ___________

17. 27:3 = ___________

18. 4:36 = ___________

19. 10:50 = ___________

20. 3:9 = ___________

21. 64:8 = ___________

22. 4:8 = ___________

23. 16:48 = ___________

24. 16:12 = ___________

Ratios: Word Problems

Solve.

1. A car can travel 85 kilometers on 17 liters of gasoline. How much gasoline will it need to go 145 kilometers?

2. 22 lbs of rice cost $66. How many lbs of rice can you get with $42 ?

3. 27 lbs of oranges cost $81. How many lbs of oranges can you get with $129 ?

4. A boat can travel 279 miles on 31 gallons of gasoline. How far can it travel on 3 gallons?

Change decimals to percents and vice versa

1. 74% = 0.74
2. 99% = 0.99
3. 53% = 0.53
4. 86% = 0.86
5. 77% = 0.77
6. 39% = 0.39
7. 11% = 0.11
8. 21% = 0.21
9. 23% = 0.23
10. 82% = 0.82
11. 69% = 0.69
12. 58% = 0.58
13. 5% = 0.05
14. 50% = 0.5
15. 63% = 0.63
16. 69% = 0.69
17. 37% = 0.37
18. 81% = 0.81
19. 72% = 0.72
20. 76% = 0.76
21. 49% = 0.49
22. 69% = 0.69
23. 65% = 0.65
24. 21% = 0.21
25. 30% = 0.3
26. 10% = 0.1
27. 13% = 0.13
28. 94% = 0.94
29. 46% = 0.46
30. 56% = 0.56
31. 44% = 0.44
32. 45% = 0.45

33. 28% = 0.28

34. 22% = 0.22

35. 9% = 0.09

36. 57% = 0.57

37. 78% = 0.78

38. 97% = 0.97

39. 55% = 0.55

40. 60% = 0.6

41. 49% = 0.49

42. 51% = 0.51

43. 77% = 0.77

44. 27% = 0.27

45. 26% = 0.26

46. 37% = 0.37

47. 31% = 0.31

48. 59% = 0.59

49. 18% = 0.18

50. 7% = 0.07

51. 71% = 0.71

52. 6% = 0.06

53. 13% = 0.13

54. 48% = 0.48

55. 92% = 0.92

56. 58% = 0.58

57. 28% = 0.28

58. 55% = 0.55

59. 3% = 0.03

60. 87% = 0.87

61. 32% = 0.32

62. 60% = 0.6

63. 16% = 0.16

64. 10% = 0.1

Find percentages of numbers

1. 50% of 110 is 55
2. 30% of 110 is 33
3. 50% of 130 is 65
4. 40% of 0 is 0
5. 60% of 150 is 90
6. 60% of 70 is 42
7. 50% of 20 is 10
8. 100% of 110 is 110
9. 80% of 80 is 64
10. 40% of 150 is 60
11. 90% of 0 is 0
12. 60% of 40 is 24
13. 70% of 0 is 0
14. 50% of 140 is 70
15. 50% of 100 is 50
16. 70% of 40 is 28
17. 70% of 40 is 28
18. 0% of 50 is 0
19. 40% of 50 is 20
20. 50% of 150 is 75
21. 10% of 90 is 9
22. 100% of 130 is 130
23. 80% of 70 is 56
24. 70% of 10 is 7
25. 50% of 10 is 5
26. 30% of 60 is 18
27. 70% of 90 is 63
28. 70% of 80 is 56
29. 70% of 30 is 21
30. 50% of 110 is 55
31. 20% of 110 is 22
32. 90% of 20 is 18

33. 100% of 66 is 66

34. 90% of 11 is 9.9

35. 100% of 106 is 106

36. 30% of 128 is 38.4

37. 30% of 72 is 21.6

38. 0% of 53 is 0

39. 10% of 136 is 13.6

40. 70% of 69 is 48.3

41. 30% of 99 is 29.7

42. 0% of 90 is 0

43. 20% of 19 is 3.8

44. 20% of 121 is 24.2

45. 90% of 134 is 120.6

46. 50% of 108 is 54

47. 90% of 148 is 133.2

48. 70% of 6 is 4.2

49. 37% of 59 is 21.83

50. 88% of 99 is 87.12

51. 90% of 26 is 23.4

52. 55% of 135 is 74.25

53. 77% of 102 is 78.54

54. 31% of 146 is 45.26

55. 48% of 111 is 53.28

56. 74% of 31 is 22.94

57. 65% of 111 is 72.15

58. 31% of 68 is 21.08

59. 42% of 146 is 61.32

60. 17% of 15 is 2.55

61. 61% of 72 is 43.92

62. 59% of 85 is 50.15

63. 33% of 54 is 17.82

64. 46% of 24 is 11.04

65. 6% of 22 is 1.32

66. 85% of 142 is 120.7

Find how many percent a number is of another

1. 50 is 50% of 100
2. 45 is 75% of 60
3. 25 is 50% of 50
4. 60 is 100% of 60
5. 10 is 12.5% of 80
6. 25 is 62.5% of 40
7. 10 is 22.222% of 45
8. 25 is 45.455% of 55
9. 50 is 83.333% of 60
10. 10 is 14.286% of 70
11. 20 is 20% of 100
12. 10 is 10.526% of 95
13. 10 is 50% of 20
14. 45 is 60% of 75
15. 5 is 16.667% of 30
16. 35 is 43.75% of 80
17. 75 is 83.333% of 90
18. 45 is 100% of 45
19. 15 is 30% of 50
20. 5 is 50% of 10
21. 70 is 70% of 100
22. 50 is 66.667% of 75
23. 5 is 9.091% of 55
24. 5 is 20% of 25
25. 15 is 17.647% of 85
26. 40 is 44.444% of 90

Percentage Worksheet Summary

1. 68% of 56 is 38.08
2. 12 is 50% of 24

3. 9 is 23.077% of 39

4. 13 is 18.056% of 72

5. 32% of 63 is 20.16

6. 8 is 10.256% of 78

7. 34 is 40% of 85

8. 27% of 86 is 23.22

9. 41% of 45 is 18.45

10. 26 is 34.211% of 76

11. 67% of 23 is 15.41

12. 70% of 26 is 18.2

13. 9% of 59 is 5.31

14. 60% of 39 is 23.4

15. 29 is 32.584% of 89

16. 54% of 21 is 11.34

17. 2 is 4.762% of 42

18. 93% of 17 is 15.81

19. 11% of 90 is 9.9

20. 78 is 78.788% of 99

21. 39 is 79.592% of 49

22. 40 is 52.632% of 76

23. 73% of 21 is 15.33

24. 63% of 40 is 25.2

25. 73% of 19 is 13.87

26. 1 is 1.087% of 92

27. 2 is 4.348% of 46

28. 49% of 61 is 29.89

29. 53 is 56.989% of 93

30. 14% of 99 is 13.86

31. 43% of 6 is 2.58

32. 8% of 79 is 6.32

33. 93% of 95 is 88.35

Reduce Ratios

1. 2:4 = 1:2
2. 6:9 = 2:3
3. 5:15 =1:3
4. 12:20 = 3:5
5. 18:45 = 2:5
6. 21:49 = 3:7
7. 33:121 = 3:11
8. 30:72 = 5:12
9. 39:52 = 3:4
10. 52:56 = 13:14
11. 90:78 = 15:13
12. 90:70 = 9:7
13. 94:96 = 47:48
14. 45:39 = 15:13
15. 92:2 = 46:1
16. 24:4 = 6:1
17. 27:3 = 3:1
18. 4:36 = 1:9
19. 10:50 = 1:5
20. 3:9 = 1:3
21. 64:8 = 8:1
22. 4:8 = 1:2
23. 16:48 = 1:3
24. 16:12 = 4:3

Ratios: Word Problems

1. 29 liters.
2. 14 lbs.
3. 43 lbs.
4. 27 miles.

www.ingramcontent.com/pod-product-compliance
Lightning Source LLC
LaVergne TN
LVHW060834170826
845678LV00010B/1976

* 9 7 9 8 8 6 9 4 5 1 5 1 4 *